Changes

Changes

By Gwen Davis

Nash Publishing • Los Angeles

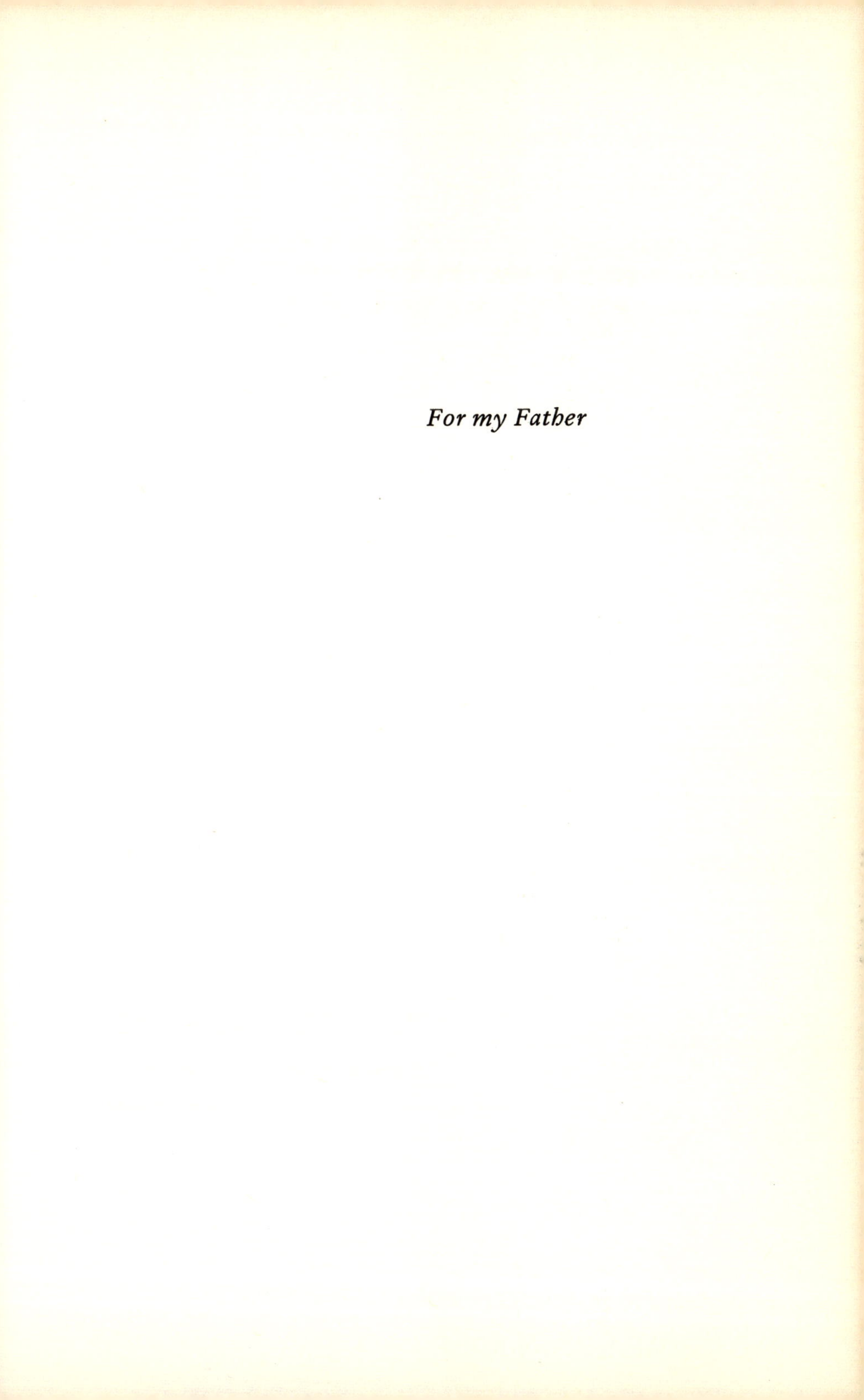

For my Father

Changes

Palm against palm
That way we can feel each other's
Fortunes;
A tender mano a mano
Pore by pore
Line by line
Heart, destiny, life
All that making love is for.
Provided
You're not a
    Scorpio. . .

I am naked
Vulnerable
Transparent
You can see through me?
How clever of you
When I have ripped my skin off.

I took my children out on the hill
To show them to God
Hedging all bets
"Good evening God," I said
    "Hello, God," said Madeleine, then four
    "Hi, God!" said Robert, recently turned two.

"We'd like to thank You for all
The blessings of the past year," I said.
    "Thank you God," said Madeleine
    "Thanks, God," said Robert miraculously turned two.

"And if we've done anything wrong
We're sorry."
    "We're really sorry, God," said Madeleine.
    "Sorry, God, it was an accident."

"Now
All that we'd like to ask
Is a break God."
    "Give us a break, God." (Madeleine)
    (Robert) "God isn't saying Hello."

Oh
What a stroke of beauty
Putting green on trees
Setting trees on hills
Arching hills against sky
Cluttered with clouds
Dripping with rain.
Fine composition
I call that
A good sense of
Balance
Of nature.

Listen
I'm your daughter
Sometimes you treat me
Like another country.

My son has asked to marry me
Finally
It took him four years.
"When I grow up
Will you marry me
and I'll say
Yes yes yes yes yes yes yes yes
All the time."
Is that the four-year-old
Concept of love:
Giving in to tyranny
Completely?

I glimpsed a perfect phrase
It has eluded me:
    A silvery fish in the
    Streamaway of thought.
I found a perfect love
It has denuded me
    Better by the love
    Than by the phrase be caught.
    (Or maybe not.)

Remember
The gray days of April
Tinged with pink
That was the hope of May
The promise of love
Around the edges of the rain.
Spring was
An adolescent season
Filled with self-doubt
And weeping
Part of it from the sky.
A few railed at the heavens
Some succumbed to melancholy
The rest moved to where
The weather was less changeable.

Where is she now
Carmen Miranda?
She really knew
How to have a good time.

Fruit on her head
Nails on her fingers
And an 8x10 glossy
To prove she wasn't in drag.

What a lot of rage was there
Wasted in our youth
What a lot of lies examined
Searching for the truth.

What a spate of rainy days
Waiting for the sun
How could there be many loves
When there wasn't one?

Corpulence and opulence
And virulence and stuff
What perspective life can give
If we live long enough.

And if you love another
Instead of only me
Where is the sorrow
Except in my ego
Where is the pain
Except imagined—
Hearts don't break,
Did you ever really hear
A heart breaking?
They lie of course
The dreamers who believe
In love
True
Eternal
All fulfilling.
I want nothing from you
Except perhaps for you to listen
And see if you can hear
The crackling of my soul.

Dad . . .
I didn't get my Batmobile at F.A.O. Schwart'
At F.A.O. Schwart'
They're all out of Batmobiles
I got it from Santa Claus,
There really is a Santa Claus
Isn't there?
There really isn't just
An F.A.O. Schwart'?

Dad . . .
Why do Batman and Robin have this
Little red thing like policemen have
On police cars
On their Batmobile
You know what I mean, this thing
Like the flashing red light
On police cars?
> "Because they represent
> Law and Order. Do you
> know what Law and Order is?"

Yeah.
> "What?"

Fighting.

Caution:
People are living
Inside those children skins
Thoughts are forming
Behind those eyes
Handle with care.

Camellias bloom
On Christmas Day
In California
Compliments of the season

Cards come
Courtesy of the garbage man

Late blossomers
Thrive
In a remedial
Glow

Too much of a good thing:
Sunshine

All year round.

Where can the sadness go
When there are no
Sewers?

Dumbo
Had a mother that got locked up
For protecting her baby
When everybody called it a freak;
Bambi
Had a mother that got burned up
 In a forest fire
Where her gentle little deer was trapped;
Snow White
Had a stepmother, wicked
(Was there ever another
Kind?)
Who wanted
The heart of the little bitch
Back from the forest
So there wouldn't be anybody
Fairer in the land;
Oh what dreams
That sweet Walt Disney gave us—
Oh my God
Was that a man who loved
Children.

For a child
The world breaks into
Kaleidoscopic prisms
White delight
Roseate hope
Yellow surprise;
Then comes time
Like a dustman
Sweeping it into a pile of
Gray.
Scatter the ashes!
There's still room for
Color here.

Madeleine

That's Lucille Ball's house
Amy Meltzer went trick-or-treating there
Hallowe'en
The man who came to the door
Said Lucille Ball wouldn't come to the door
Because she doesn't want anyone to see her
That's what Amy Meltzer says.
When I have my Birthday can I invite her?
                    "Amy Meltzer?"
Yes. And also Lucille Ball.

Robert

A Visit to San Francisco

I want to show Rickey my Dad
(Rickey lives next door
To the house where we're being
Houseguests.)
Da-ad? DA—AD!
(stomping up the stairs)
He went to a football game?
In Real Life?
He wouldn't do that
Not without me
You lie!
(to dog—lifting up its ears)
Don't like my mother!
(to me)
Why are you laughing?
He has ears!
You think these ears are for nothing?
(stomping back down the stairs)
Rickey? Rickey?
I want you to meet my Dad.
This is my Dad.
(pointing to the air)
My Dad's invisible.

Why didn't we
Have the guts
That merciless August
Drenched with the heat of sun
And innocence
To say:
"Here's who I am.
Here's how I feel."

Spin the night round with a silvery thread
Weaving it into a bright cocoon for morning
And let the day emerge from its own shadow
Radiant.

Step
Along with step
That's how we should take it
Not
Step by step
Not a step behind,
Let's get energy
Basking in each other's dignity
Once we can step out like that
We can skip.

Some you win
And some you win by default
Simply by being around
When the battle is over.

What, angry my love?
Speakst thou with filter tips?
Heated words
Blazing rage
What a waste of good breath.

Let's not struggle for clues
Guess at each other's motives:
Let's bring it all out at the start of the piece
And then we can know who the Murderer is
Before the crime takes place.

Naturally
We haven't been here before
But I remember
Places I've never seen
Time unrecorded;
And your skin touching mine
Feverish and cold
By slow and fast degrees
That I remember
Along with the Nile.

Pay no attention
To poisonous spiders
Even if they're in your bed
And far from their native country.
There is such a thing as odd coincidence
And no need for paranoia.

Here
Where the light is dimmest
Let us forage among the leaves
Of rained-on love
Searching
For some persistent bud
Dormant only for winter
Darkness
And disbelief.

No lies between us—
A presumptuous request
On my part
A bountiful gift on yours.
Indian giver.

Robert

How come Mommys have such soft skin
On the inside of their arms
Because they're so old?

              I'm not so old.

YOUR FACE IS GOLD!!!
(squeezing my cheeks)
That's like a rhyme
You're not so old
Your face is gold
Is that like a rhyme?

              That's like a rhyme.

I'm hungry
I'm thirsty
Can I have some
Orange juice and
Cheese
Please.
That's like rhyme?

              That's like a rhyme.

I love you.

              That's like a rhyme.

Play
In a brighter key
Your sad, disappointed song
Give it a little less bass
A bit more pedal
And a better chance.

There are people
Who fight over
Games.
How would they be in a war?
Do the people
Who make the wars
Relax with
Games?

Once we walked in a sandy cove
And listened to whispers of sea
Watched the stars glisten, and said that life
Was whatever we willed it to be.

Now you don't know my married name
And I haven't a clue where you are.
The ocean has washed our young footprints away
Drills and spillage have cloaked them with tar.

Still, life is an upper, I firmly believe
Spiting pain, disappointment, and toil—
Perhaps we may not see the face of God
But we could speak to Standard Oil.

Where are they
All those campus activists?
I heard the youth vote
Didn't show up at the polls.
Where are the ones in sweatshirts
With hope in their hearts
At student meetings
Fiercely determined
Not to let the world

26

Go to hell.
Here we are
All grown up—some say older—
Sitting in the kitchen
Drinking coffee.
Well
At least we voted.

But I know
There are those murmurs of
Ancient sailors
Beguiled by a song
Lured onto treacherous rocks.
That was so long ago
Don't be afraid to listen.
And may I borrow your comb?

Anger
Is such a waste
Of all the heartbeats
You could use for
Love.
Not to mention
The adrenalin.

Robert is a worm at the moment
"Not an inchworm," he says
"The kind of worms that dogs get."
At the moment he is thirty-eight inching
Along the floor
Trying to get the dog
The kind of dog that worms get.

I can feel us
Whirling through
Time together,
Something softer than wind
Playing on our
Backs
Strumming us gently
Raising us into song.

A flaw
Serves the better to set off
Perfection;
That is the reason
For anguish in joy
And the origin
Of Jewish guilt.

To feel the wind as something stronger than air
To feel the earth as something more than beginning and during
    and end
To feel the silence, to listen with the skin
To feel your skin as something apart from flesh against mine
That would be something to feel
That would really be
Something.

See
How with my love tied behind my back
I still reach out to you
With my eyes.
Are they too honest for you?
Am I?

Love is a good exercise
For memory
Caught while the eye for detail
Still blinks
Stored in fine recollection
Put on display now and again
So it doesn't become
Antique

Catch me
We are so temporary
Take hold of me
And feel how
Here I am.

Whirl me
Like the leaf I would like to become
Borne on a constantly changing wind.

Let's not dwell in the past
The layers of vanished dreams
Have vast striations
Of fossilized bones
Crushed in with memory.
Not that we should live for the moment
But let's at least
Feel it go by.

I have a friend
With no illusions
She tells me,
So she's never been disappointed
She says.
She's about fifty pounds overweight
And she snorts cocaine on weekends;
But she's never been disappointed
She never had
Any illusions.

Robert

Can I touch the sky
When I grow up?
I'll be bigger than Daddy
Daddy can touch the ceiling—
Pick me up
Help me reach for it now.
No. Not the ceiling.
The sky.

Madeleine

On my birthday
Can we go to Geniiland
And they'll put a crown on my head
And a king's robes
And everybody'll watch me
And Daddy can drive all the
Children in the class
And you can hold the dog
Because I'll be very busy
Having a crown on my head?

It would be easy
Toeing in
Testing the water of love
With tiny extremities
Pulling away from cold.
I prefer plunging
Very refreshing
There's good exercise in
Joyous commitment
Some danger of drowning of course
But how very dry
The safe land of timidity
Seems.

There are some people
Who don't even understand
Pity.
Don't waste it on them.

That was the summer
We hid behind the barn
Even though we weren't farm girls
Because it was the season to "apprentice"
To learn a craft . . .
An art . . .
The theatre.
Spending our parents' money to live
In poverty, near Stamford, Connecticut.
Painting a flat, yes, please, I can do the part
With the record
Get you some coffee
Talent bursts these fat jeans
Can you tell?
Can you imagine?
Are you really in the Actor's Studio
And were you called before the Committee
And do you know . . . do you even suspect
Marlon Brando?
I met him once. Twice. Three times.
I recognized him instantly
Someone beautiful who could hurt me
Even though he had nothing against me
Personally.

Those people had affairs.
With men. Married men

But very big on
Broadway
Say nothing.
What monumental secrets they could tell me
Because they spoke so well
In voices that sounded like brains.

But I still went behind the barn
With J.D. Salinger
Because he told me in a day
What feelings we adolescents have
Even when we are turning
Slightly middle-aged.
They think that's dated now,
The Catcher in the Rye
But then, so are we.
So is Marlon Brando
Who, I suspect
Was sure he had been born to play
Holden Caulfield
And still could, inside his face
It's only on the outside we are cast
In older roles.
There is no summer stock
To work out the kinks in confusion.

There are some who despise
The innocent eye
Those with the scratches on
Their fantasies.

There is a brilliant moon shining
In my love's face
Brightening darkness for me
Streaming a ray of laughter
On the pain.
Werewolves could rampage by that light.
So can I.

Can't we lick at each other's
Flames
Feed fire with fire
No need to consume
Or be extinguished
By apathy.

Mommy
Do you know how it feels
On television and on boxes?
I mean how it feels to be talking
On television and on boxes
How does it feel?
How does it feel to be
Not in Real Life?

Wounding
Is the lazy way
Take my flesh in gentle hands
My mouths in yours
Heal. Heal.

I have more sense
In my whole body
Than you have
In your little finger.
Want to see?
Taste
Hear
Smell
Feel.

40

When
Footsteps shy of seeking mercy,
All that we reach for is the wispy feather of chance
Satin bows on our spirit, why don't we dance?
It worked for Ann Miller.

I had different plans
Involving Tahiti
Living among coconut palms
Perhaps with one ear.
And here you are
Setting me inside a house
With all my features on,
Trailing a duo of glory.

Our dog
Rolls over and plays
Alive.

Robert

Why do people
Throw garbage
In the water
Don't they know
It kills the fishes?
I know
Let's go through the ocean
And clean it all up
There's no school today
Let's unpollute.

To Eskimos
Heaven is earth warm to walk on,
To desert tribes
A place where oases never end.
What luxury we live in
To dream of
Peace
Love
Understanding.
What innocent primitives dwell
In split-level
Consciousness.

What's a horizon?
           It's everything you can see meeting the sky
           There's a tree on your horizon
           There's a hill...
There's a telephone pole!
           There's everything in the world on your
               horizon
           You're six years old.
Mostly I see buildings.

Gloria Mundi
Table-top dancer
World traveler
Eighth-grade SDS member

Married Republican
Moved to the suburbs
Breast-fed her children
Sic transit Gloria

Thoreau said
"Simplify."
I wish he were here
To help me with
The garage sale.

Robert is four
And he can tear a leaf apart
With his bare hands
He would take on any deer
In Japanese Village.
"Come on, put up your Dupes," he says.
He is somewhat more friendly
To lions and tigers.

A Theosophic Discussion Between Two Children

Why doesn't God say 'What?'
When I ask a question?
When I call Him
Why doesn't he say 'What?'
When I call anybody else
They say 'What'
Why doesn't God say 'What?'

Call him again.

Go--od, Go--od!

What?

I propose
A Children's Liberation:
Some of us can canvass
The neighborhoods
Surveying the becauses
So we can answer all the unasked whys.

Why do I have to listen?
Why obey
Such direct orders:
Go here
Go there
Do this
Don't do that
Not in the living room.
What have I done
That I am in jail?
Oppressed
Drafted.
Why are we even at war?

I didn't ask to join
What did I do wrong—
Except be born
Young.

There are some places
Good people shouldn't have to go:
To the grave
To a party with no laughs
To a room
Where everybody's Republican.

When I was one and twenty
I'd heard a poem say
'Give pounds and crowns and guineas
But not your heart away.'

Now I am over thirty
And I have wept a bit
But those who counsel not to trust
Are really full of shit.

Look
I love you
Sometimes we don't say
Exactly what we mean
Don't listen
Look

Once I went with my family
To the Sixth Avenue Delicatessen
And Cesar Romero
Sat eating a roast beef on rye
With coleslaw and Russian dressing.
He took a bite
And nothing fell out
He chewed
And after every swallow
He wiped his mouth
With a napkin.
When he was finished
My mother reached over
And slapped my step-father's face.

When we are young
We wait for the phone to ring
So someone can tell us
They are in love;
When we are older
We are still waiting
For the phone to ring
So someone can tell us
We have a job
Or we are useful
Or there's good news
Somewhere.
Oh God! The agony
Wrought by optimism
Dreams of romance
Alexander Graham Bell
And upward mobility.

Moe, Shemp, and Larry.
Green shelly citizens
Of Florida
Came to our house
To be pets.
For a six-year-old
Who didn't like touching
Slimy
One little girl learned
To play
To let their scaly feet run on her arm
To watch them crawling loose
On the lawn
To kiss their cold wet faces.
The Doctor said
Some turtles carry salmonella
We told the little girl
They had to go
Sobbing, bereft
She wailed her worst goodbye
And set the house in shadow
With her grief.
There is no loss
Like first love
Except first turtles.

The original dream
Includes a lagoon
Diving for pearls
Surfacing to kiss
The beloved sun-watered face.
One ends up with a Mai-Tai
At Trader Vic's.

I promised my friend Sean
A poem
About a cat named Tuna
I couldn't reach Rod McKuen
So here it is, Sean.

Future Shock

Mom . . .
You know why the Red Baron's
Is called the Red Baron?
Because they spilled red paint on it.
Before it was the Gold Baron
Because it was Gold.
I'm not kidding you,
What's misinformation?
There was a man called the Red Baron?
Did they spill paint on him?
A baron was a what? Like a prince?
What's a title?
Oh.
I don't care about that.
What do you know about airplanes?

Well, here we are
Caught right in the middle
Stuck in the swinging doors
Of the building where Doubt has its offices
Leaving the unstructured madness of Hope
Parked at the curb

The harsh terrain of love
Yields grassy fields
Among the rocks
Gentle streams
For soaking
Minor wounds
From too much seeking.
Cliffs, of course
To hang from
Never knowing
If rescue's coming
But often a branch
To hoist yourself by
Sometimes even a hand
To raise you to level ground.
So much uncharted territory,
Considering the explorers
The records are sketchy
The path unsure
But well worth the risk
According to some survivors.

The Christmas People
Feel a drop in their
Joy pressure
When the signs start going up
Telling what to give him
Or what she really wants
For less than
Twenty-nine ninety-five;
They get no buzz
From decorations
That mean it's another Christmas.

The Christmas People
Go to parties
Late at night
Deep into December
Where they observe the action
From the corners of their eyes;
Watching the tide of human affairs
Go out
To see who's left over
For New Year's.

The girls read Cosmopolitan
The men read Playboy
And both advise
The Christmas People
To stay cool
And go to someplace off the beaten track

Like Yugoslavia
So they can find someone
To stay home with
Next Christmas.

A children's crusade
The battle rages
Through Memorial Day
The Fourth of July
The end of summer
Thanksgiving for what?
Where is the hopeful season?
Why do they call them
Holidays?
The lonely have
No celebrations.

I am not afraid
To reach for you
The worst you can do is
Turn away;
The best could happen
You might take hold of me
Happy possibilities
Are not to be excluded
There are worse things
Than someone turning away:
Never seeing the face
To begin with.

It doesn't come in a purple flash
As they led us to believe:
Love.
Pain comes in flashes
Love comes in on very quiet days
And doesn't even tell you it's there.
It waits
It has great patience
A good sense of humor
So it has a fine time
Laughing at you
Not even knowing
It's there.
But that's real love.

Real love is in no hurry.
Real love
Has all the time in the world.

Caryl Chessman

Oh what a cruel wind whipped up
Outside San Quentin—
Those were the things vigils were made of
Cold cruel winds.
"Hundreds of students protesting
Underneath the trees," the radio said.
The announcer wasn't present
Nor were the trees
Nor were the hundreds of students,
Only some of us
On a naked hill
Hoping they wouldn't kill him.
All night we huddled, held hands, wept, insisted
No way that he would die
No way. No way.
A sandwich truck arrived at five-thirty
A.M. To celebrate
The beginning of day, I suppose.

The marchers came and bought Hershey bars
From the sandwich truck.

A few optimists arrived
Hoping for a stay of execution.
Or something.
They waited until just past eight
To drop the pellets
The sandwich truck ran out of coffee
It was just as well.
If he had to go he might as well have gone
While there was still
Something to warm us.
It wasn't all wasted
Some of us found lovers.
The victim is so incidental.

Cats

Stalking malevolently
Shining reflecting eyes
With nothing in them
But other people's lights,
Hissing
Arching
Throwing up furballs;
I have nothing against them—
It's just that I'm allergic.

In the South of France the pretty people gathered
To try to find something to say
Or someone to say it,
On terraces that overlooked the sea
Musicians played at private parties
Where no one danced.
But young girls' dresses rustled in the wind
Chiffon sails.

There was a girl there, twenty-five
A tall dark beauty
Her eyes set so wide
You knew she could believe
And had believed so many of these people.
"You should have seen her when she was young"
They said,
The builders of empires.

Some were sent down to Calvary
Some raped, some canonized
And for the ones who loved their men
Football was televised.

Pity the poor
Male chauvinist pig
Sitting at dinner
Regarding the enemy.
Thinking in terms
Of conquest
And combat
And contests.
It isn't a contest,
I swear—
My soul on it.
Contests are too hard.
Somebody loses
Nobody likes to lose.
Why don't we just
Call it a tie
From the beginning
Join me.
Don't just sit there
Glazed,
An apple in your mouth.

—But they often make contracts
With girls who wear contacts.

Reality
Is life
With the shit kicked
Into it.

Solomon Grundy
Practised yoga on Monday
Wrote haiku on Tuesday
Went to group on Wednesday
Self-realized on Thursday
Smoked dope on Friday
Read the papers on Saturday
O.D.ed on Sunday
Poor Solomon Grundy.

My Last Housekeeper

That's my last housekeeper sitting on the shelf
Looking as if she wants to help. Myself
That wasn't the impression that I got
My husband's Instamatic that smile caught
A wonderful machine. It has the power
To catch a taste of sweet, e'er all goes sour.
She was here two weeks. I did all the cleaning
She found domestic helping too demeaning.
There was one once. I can remember
She came to us the 2nd of September
She loved to cook, and taught my babies French
"Bon nuit, Maman!" they said. She climbed a bench
And washed the windows. "Please get down," I said;
"Let me bring you a tray. Some wine? In bed?"
I gave her all my clothes, my heart, my word,
She stayed until September twenty-third
When she was due back to teach at Montessori.
She hadn't told me that part of the story
During her interview. She only said
She wanted someone kind. Not someone dead.
Who'd stoop to blame her? Just because she lied
And said she'd stay forever, and I died?
Only for two weeks, then I got Maxine
Mad about babies, couldn't wait to clean
We were the only folks she loved to stay with
She gave the babies plastic bags to play with.
Margaret was cheerful, tidy, even gay,
Scotch, which was all she drank. I called AA
They sent a choreographer named Claire

To float her from our home. What say you there?
Didn't I know she drank? She didn't say . . .
Even the while they poured her to AA.
She only said "These people think I'm drunk!"
As she was climbing into Claire's car trunk.
Ten of them ripped me off. What blush bespeaks
My cheek?—If they had stayed but past three weeks,
I wouldn't have minded that much. Then I hired
A former P.R. lady who was tired
Of making it in a man's world—well I knew!
She was organic. She made seaweed stew,
Claimed we were trying to poison her, and such;
None of it did I mind, nay, not that much.
She cut the back of our garage clean off
With the side of our car. Do I mark you scoff?
Not I! I kept her till she sued
Us for whiplash. Do you think me rude?
She asked as I drove her to the bus depot
Why I was letting such a good friend go.
What say you now, employment agency?
Do you have someone tippy-top for me?
Try to remember whate'er I've been through:
Eighty-one ladies. Is it eighty-two?
I'll pay commission. Anything. One quick glance
At Anneka. We paid her way from France
She stayed with us—oh—half a day
And took off with her secret fiance.

Some part of our souls
Must remain childish
Or we would lose
The courage to keep them.

Robert

Why does the city down there
Look like that
Like a Christmas tree
Who's dead?
Is that what Los Angeles means—
Where the Christmas trees go
When they die?

Touch me
It hurts out there
Maybe your hands can't change things
But they help assuage the pain.
May I touch you
Gently
Isn't it lucky
We're both here?
That's more than most people have.

The Summer of '59

He said my eyes were so beautiful
I must have something in them;
He looked at my hands, and my breasts, and my words
As if he were bound to win them.

He wooed me with wit, and charm, and quotes
Of erotica, intellectual;
And he was the moon, and the stars, and the sky
And totally homosexual.

A tender wind
Brushes against you
With as much love
As gentle people give.
Normally
This would be known as
Pathetic Fallacy
Especially
To the people who've never allowed themselves
To ride
The wind.

Home Town

I really believe
Tap dancing
Originated
In Pittsburgh

If you moved fast enough
You could get out of there.

Why did they put
Metal on my sole?
I like the sound
But I miss my Grandma.

Now
As if this were the last time
Move your lips on my face
While I touch mine to you
Slowly
As if to memorize
Skin we will never touch again
Record my mouth
Receive my loving overflow
Remember lightly
As if it were the last time—
And I will study you
As if it were the first.

Robert

I plucked him from the ceiling
Of a chapel,
A Greco-Roman cherub
A little too noisy for the room.

Madeleine

She is so long and lithe for six
Her hair is on straight
And she kisses people.
She knows she is not supposed
To talk to strangers
So she kisses them.

When the dream dies
When the courage you had
Late in the day
That allowed you to continue
Into night, hoping
The wonder might be there tomorrow,
When that dream vanishes
It is easy
To watch
The ABC Movie of the Week

Come
Sit beside me
Warm yourself
At my fire
Let's toast
Marshmallow feelings
Crisp on the outside
Wet, sweet, soft
Within:
You be a Boy Scout
I'll be a Campfire Girl
And we will believe
In the simplicity of
Groupsing
Forest rangers
Summer evenings
And love.

Weeds, too,
Have a belligerent beauty
Growing unattended
Ripped from the statelier gardens
Forming insistent designs
On the runaway landscapes.

We went to a meeting last night
Of those who plan to subdivide Mars,
Realtors mainly
And some synergistic conversionists.

He of course
Is Albert Einstein
She is Florence Nightingale
They just happen to be
Watching the Three Stooges
At the moment.

I
Lie to you?
After all we have said of truth?
Of the innocence that passes passion
In its energy.
I
Lie to you?
After how we have touched
After all we have seen
And laughed at
That no one understands
But you and
I
Lie to you?
It's possible.

Watermelon emotions
Are good in summer
And your fifteenth year
When things should be
A little sweet
And empty
And full of pits.

Decadence
Such an elegant word
Perhaps if we changed it
To "Splat."
Sybarite
Quite a lofty description
Of those who seek pleasure,
Strictly.
Could we alter it to "Trel"?
Who could aspire
To being a Trel
Living in Splat?

The color of change is
Sadness
Speckled with brilliant green
A bright contradiction
Laughter around the edges
Eating away like acid
At the asinine.

Do you remember
When reminiscing
Was about the time you met
At the edge of the lake
And the way the water looked
All still and innocent
As you were unwilling to be
Very much longer
And not who played Sam Spade's partner in
The Maltese Falcon?

That is a time
Sunset
Even on days
When there is no sun,
Watching the brilliant insistence
Of light and life
As told by red geraniums
Fade into darkness
Move into sheer imagination
That is a specter-y,
Here-comes-yesterday
Time.

Of course those of us who were
Royalists in our dreams
The ones with the Prince in them
(You remember *those*)
Were socialists in the daytime
Shedding tears for the oppressed
Which included ourselves
With the way we were treated
By them
(You remember *them*).
That's the way the world was
In the Age of Sex and Social Consciousness
When you thought of nothing but
Him
And the rest of the world.

Of course those of us who were
Victorian in behavior
Where you'd only let him go
So far
(You remember how far so far was)
Were hedonists in our fantasies
The ones that we didn't dare have
So we woke ourselves up
And thought of
Starvation in India
And what was he doing now?

Skipping around the puddles
On sinister sidewalks
Can help you avoid
Wet-footed despair.
Sadness in nature
Doesn't exists
Except in holocaust;
No need to seek
Reflected sorrow
In willows weeping.
A most unnatural disaster:
Unloving love.

Kisses
Alter only the mouth's
Consistency
Softening it
Into caring
And probing
And sweet persistence

Kisses
Only make the lips
Moister
More giving
More seeking
More yielding
In tender combat

Fluttering the tongue
Aiming at the heart.

They cannot
Change the shape of the words.

PICTORIAL SOURCES

The photographs on the following pages were taken by Don Mitchell: 33, 34, 45, 48, 64, 72, 75.

The photographs on the following pages were taken by Chuck Pendergast: 6, 13, 16, 42, 51.